My Pumpkin

Written by Julia Noonan

Illustrated by Peter Lawson

children's press ®

A Division of Scholastic Inc.

New York Toronto London Auckland Sydney
Mexico City New Delhi Hong Kong
Danbury, Connecticut

Library of Congress Cataloging-in-Publication Data

Noonan, Julia.
  My pumpkin / by Julia Noonan ; illustrated by Peter Lawson.
      p. cm. — (My first reader)
  Summary: A young boy plants and grows pumpkins, taking one of them to the fair.
  ISBN 0-516-24876-6 (lib. bdg.)   0-516-24973-8 (pbk.)
  [1. Pumpkins—Fiction. 2. Stories in rhyme.] I. Lawson, Peter, ill. II. Title. III. Series.
  PZ8.3.N7445Myap 2005
  [E]—dc22
                                    2005004027

Text © 2005 Nancy Hall, Inc.
Illustrations © 2005 Peter Lawson
All rights reserved.
Published in 2005 by Children's Press, an imprint of Scholastic Library Publishing.
Published simultaneously in Canada.
Printed in the United States of America.

1 2 3 4 5 6 7 8 9 10 R 14 13 12 11 10 09 08 07 06 05

Note to Parents and Teachers

Once a reader can recognize and identify the 48 words used to tell this story, he or she will be able to successfully read the entire book. These 48 words are repeated throughout the story, so that young readers will be able to recognize the words easily and understand their meaning.

The 48 words used in this book are:

a	hole	me	round	them
ball	I	my	row	this
big	in	one	seeds	time
by	is	out	show	to
dig	it	outside	small	very
fall	it's	plant	spring	water
from	judge	prize	start	weeds
gives	lay	pull	surprise	won
go	like	pumpkin	take	
grow	lot	pumpkins	the	

It's spring outside.

It's time to go!

I lay my seeds out in a row.

I dig a hole.

9

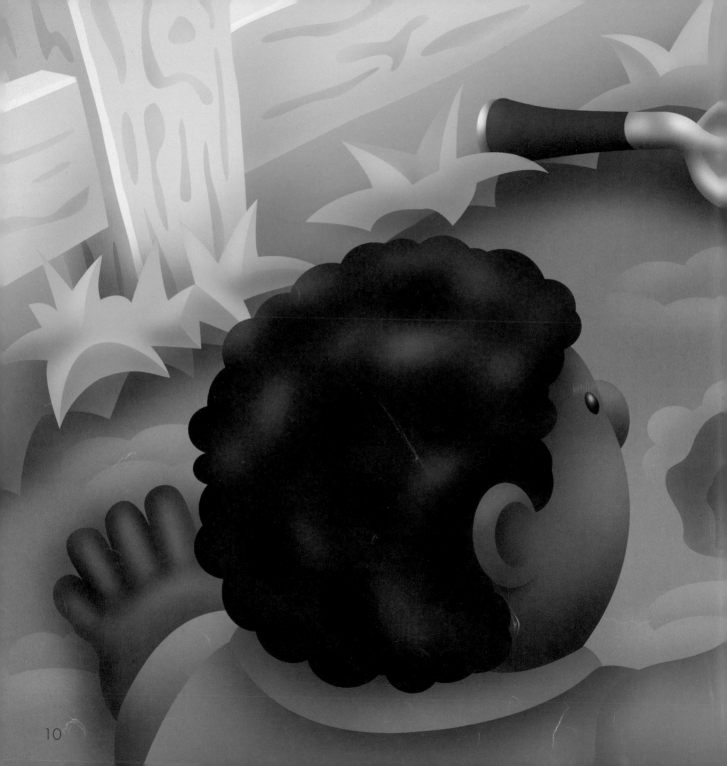

I plant the seeds.

I water them.

I pull the weeds.

My pumpkins start out very small.

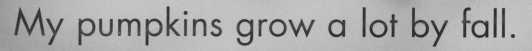

My pumpkins grow a lot by fall.

This one is big.

This one is small.

This one is round. It's like a ball!

I take one pumpkin from the row.

I take it to the pumpkin show.

The judge gives me a big surprise.

My pumpkin won!

I won a prize!

ABOUT THE AUTHOR

Julia Noonan has written and illustrated stories for as long as she can remember. She began writing her first published book, *Hare and Rabbit: Friends Forever,* while in the fifth grade. Her favorite kids books by other authors are *Dr. DeSoto* and *A Bargain for Frances.* Julia loves animals. She and her daughter Anna share a gentle Doberman named Raja.

ABOUT THE ILLUSTRATOR

Peter Lawson has been illustrating children's books for almost 20 years. Before that, he spent three years building rowing boats for racing. Peter lives in the United Kingdom with his wife Karen, their daughter Thea (who believes that all Peter does is eat biscuits and color), as well as their three cats, two rabbits, and a pony.